Edition Schott

Krzysztof Penderecki

1933–2020

Aria

aus „3 Stücke im alten Stil"
arrangiert für Klavier solo von Tim Allhoff (2020)
nach dem Original für Streichorchester (1963)

from "Three Pieces in Old Style"
arranged for piano solo by Tim Alhoff (2020)
based on the original version for string orchestra (1963)

ED 23426
ISMN 979-0-001-21267-0

Ebenfalls erhältlich / Also available:
Originalfassung / Original version
CON 241
ISMN 979-0-001-02505-8 (Partitur / Full score)

Fassung für gemischten Chor a cappella / Version for mixed choir a cappella
C 56532
ISMN 979-0-001-20043-1

www.schott-music.com

Mainz · London · Madrid · Paris · New York · Tokyo · Beijing
© 2020 Schott Music GmbH & Co. KG, Mainz · Printed in Germany

Ersteinspielung / First recording:
OKEH (SONY MUSIC) 9463845
Tim Alhoff: Sixteen Pieces for Piano
Tim Alhoff, Klavier / piano

Dauer / Duration: 2'

Vorwort

Krzysztof Pendereckis *Aria* begegnete mir erstmals in einer Folge der Netflix-Serie „Black Mirror".
Das Stück hat mich vom ersten Moment gefesselt und ich war bei der Recherche sehr überrascht,
dass es sich nicht um ein barockes Werk handelt, sondern um eine Komposition Pendereckis, den
ich eher als Komponisten moderner, zeitgenössischer klassischer Musik verortet hatte. Ich fand
später heraus, dass *Aria* den ersten Satz seiner *3 Stücke im alten Stil* bildet – einen Zyklus, den der
Komponist für den Film „Die Handschrift von Saragossa" geschrieben hat.
Da ich Pendereckis Musik und Klangsprache schon immer bewundert und mich, vor allen Dingen
pianistisch, viel mit der Musik des Barock beschäftigt habe, kamen zwei Dinge zusammen und ich
wollte die *Aria* unbedingt für Klavier transkribieren und im Rahmen der zeitgleich stattfindenden
Produktion meines Albums „Sixteen Pieces for Piano" aufnehmen.
Das Stück zeichnet sich durch seine einfache Schönheit aus, die direkt „ins Herz" geht. Besonders
den Übergang von Dur nach Moll in Takt 9 auf 10 schätze ich sehr.

Tim Alhoff

Preface

I first heard Krzysztof Penderecki's *Aria* in an episode of the Netflix series "Black Mirror". The
piece fascinated me from the very first moment, and while researching it, I was very surprised
to discover that it was not a baroque work, but instead a composition by Penderecki, whom
I had rather seen as a composer of modern, contemporary classical music. I later found out
that *Aria* is the first movement of his *3 Stücke im alten Stil* [Three pieces in old style] – a cycle
that the composer wrote for the film "The Saragossa Manuscript".
Since I have always admired Penderecki's music and tonal language and, especially as a pianist,
have taken great interest in baroque music, these two things added up to my wanting to transcribe
Aria for piano and record it as part of the simultaneous production of my album "Sixteen Pieces
for Piano".
The piece is characterized by its simple beauty, which goes straight "to the heart". I especially
appreciate the transition from major to minor in bars 9-10.

Tim Alhoff
(Translation: Paul Schäffer)

Aria

Krzysztof Penderecki
1933–2020
Arr.: Tim Allhoff

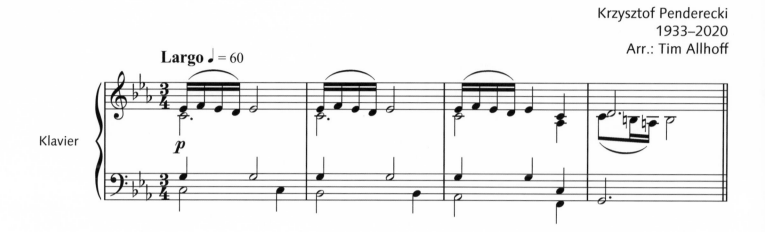

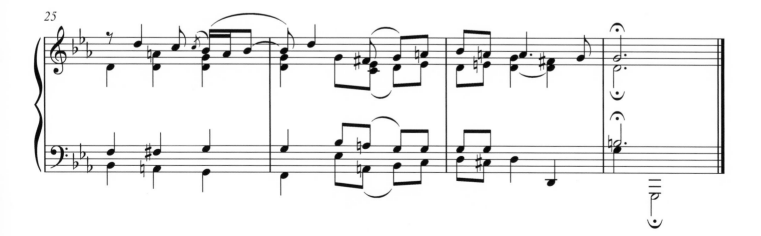

Schott Music, Mainz 59 908